LETTERS TO AFRICA

Dedicated to our friends in Africa

First published by uclanpublishing, 2010

Publishing House, Media Factory,
University of Central Lancashire,
Preston, Lancashire
PR1 2HE

ISBN 13: 9780956528315

LETTERS TO AFRICA

With contributions from bestselling authors
Lauren St John, Mary Hoffman and
Ifeoma Onyefulu

ZAMBIA 2d

UNITED KINGDOM AM
12345 2010

KENYA, AFRICA PM
12798 2010

6d
KENYA, AFRICA PM
12798 2010

uclanpublishing

University of Central Lancashire

Welcome to Letters to Africa,

What do we think of when we think of "Africa"? We are bombarded with a multitude of often conflicting representations. Rarely do we catch a glimpse of what the people who live in this vibrant continent really think and feel.

In publishing this book we are hoping to bridge the cultural divide between UK and African schoolchildren by giving them a chance to tell us about their lives through letters, drawings and photographs.

The project began whilst I was on a visit to the University of Central Lancashire's Maasai Centre in Kimana, Kenya, last year. I was struck by the vibrancy and zest of the schoolchildren and brilliance of the teachers in the area, despite a long drought, which had left the land parched and the people hungry. They were eager to learn skills that would enable them to develop their communities: engineering, construction, sustainability and alternative power. All of this they did in make-shift classrooms of corrugated iron.

I thought we had so much to learn from them and was determined to conceive a project that would be an excellent learning and cultural experience for students and teachers in the UK and Africa, and would also raise some funds to purchase educational resources for the schools we visited in Africa. Letters to Africa was born.

It has been a wonderful experience for all involved. Students from multiple disciplines at the University of Central Lancashire have come together with teachers and schoolchildren in Kenya and Zambia to provide you with a unique and, we hope, engaging, publication. We have learned so much from each other, not least that we have so much in common despite many obvious differences. All the profits will go towards purchasing resources for the children in Africa featured in this book. We hope you will enjoy it as much as we have.

Debbie Williams,
Head of uclanpublishing
DJWilliams1@uclan.ac.uk

CONTENTS

Introduction by Lauren St John   1
Dear Reader   4
From Jack to Solomon   6
The Real Africa by Mary Hoffman   9

Letters about Home   13
It's Not Like Where I'm From   25
Letters about School   31
Kiano's Choice   45
Letters about Animals   51
Why Do Monkeys Live Up Trees?   67
Letters about Games and Sports   73
Let's Play   87
Letters about Food   93
Grandma's Birthday Meal   107
Let's Say Thank You by Ifeoma Onyefulu   115
Maasai Culture   118
Maa Glossary   127

Features:
Maasai Centre for Field Studies   130
South Lakes Wild Animal Park   134
Sport in Action   136

Contributors   139

Gemma Nolan

LETTERS TO AFRICA

Introduced by Lauren St John, author of *The White Giraffe*

Whenever I recall my childhood in Africa, the thing I remember most vividly is the freedom my sister and I enjoyed. We grew up on a 1,000 acre farm at the height of Zimbabwe's civil war and rarely went anywhere without a gun, and yet ironically we had more freedom, in terms of where and how we could play, than almost any child growing up in the United Kingdom today.

Faced with a variety of extreme dangers, from bullets to wildlife, our parents had to trust us and trust that we'd be okay. As a result, we spent long, happy days swimming with our dogs in the crocodile-infested river in front of our house; fording our weir – a sort of mini Victoria Falls – in full flood: riding our horses through thick bush, lying in the smooth, flexible boughs of the mulberry trees in the back yard and gorging on mulberries until our stomachs ached and our faces were bright purple.

One hundred acres of our farm was a game reserve, in which we kept our pet giraffe, two bad-tempered ostriches, a mad wildebeest, an eccentric goat who loved boats and sixty impala antelope. I spent hundreds of blissful hours painting there, or leaning against trees, reading adventure novels about children in England who slept on beds of heather and chased smugglers across fog-wreathed moors.

To me, their lives sounded incredibly exciting – much more exciting than mine – even though I had a pet giraffe and two pet warthogs called Miss Piggy and Bacon, and drove to school with an Uzi submachine gun on my lap.

In the seventies, Rhodesia, as Zimbabwe was then known, had sanctions imposed on it. That meant we were severely restricted when it came to travel and the kind of music, books and sweets that were available in the shops, and we were always deeply envious of anyone who got to go to the UK, because they came back with amazing chocolate, records and cool posters of our favourite bands.

The other thing I remember about the Africa of my childhood was the abundance. The perfect weather and rich, loamy soil caused everything to burst with life. Cows produced great drums of creamy milk, fruit trees sagged under the weight of their produce, chickens practically sang they were so happy to lay eggs.

Life in both Africa and the UK is very different now. Because of drought or war, many children in Africa grow up hungry, never knowing when they might see their next meal. Some are forced to become soldiers. For millions, school is only a dream. In the UK, few children will ever enjoy the kind of freedom my sister and I took for granted, because society has changed and schools and parents quite rightly protect them very closely.

But in both places things have changed for the better, too. In the UK, many more children are able to have a fantastic education and go on to university. They're learning that it's important to care about people and animals in far-off places like Kenya and Zambia, because the environment affects us all. In Zambia and Kenya, more children are growing up to be teachers, artists and leaders. Thanks to modern technology, more are able to communicate across continents.

This project, *Letters to Africa*, shows what a difference it can make if we just reach out to one another and try to learn from one another. A problem shared is, as they say, a problem halved. It costs nothing to care.

DEAR READER,

Last year, on a fieldtrip to the Maasai Centre for Field Studies in Kenya, UCLan Publishing manager Debbie Williams asked the centre's staff what the schools in the local area needed the most and the answer was teaching resources. After much planning and the arrival of UCLan's first ever class of fresh-faced Publishing MA students, what would eventually become the charity project *Letters to Africa* was born.

The book has been brought together by the Publishing students with input from students in many disciplines, including Writing for Children, Photography, Linguistics, Illustrators and Sports. We have also been lucky enough to have contributions from internationally renowned writers, Lauren St John, Mary Hoffman and Ifeoma Onyefulu. Even more central to this project has been the extraordinary, the funny and the heartfelt, letters between schoolchildren in the UK and Africa.

Letters to Africa has given schoolchildren from the UK, Zambia and Kenya the opportunity to ask each other the questions they've always wanted to ask, but never had the chance to before. From 'What's the scariest animal you've ever seen?' to 'What's the most embarrassing thing you've ever done?' Their boundary-crossing correspondence can only be found here, between the pages of *Letters to Africa*, the fun, bold and insightful guide to life in two continents.

There is so much to discover inside *Letters to Africa*; you will find cultural anecdotes and little known facts about the Maasai tribe, you'll learn the language of the famous Maasai (for the first time in print!), read stories by authors who have swapped fireside tales with the Maasai people and behold breathtaking photography, and it is all completely exclusive to this stunning volume.

And the best part? All profits generated from *Letters to Africa* will go towards buying vital teaching resources so that the schoolchildren taking part in Africa can carry on enjoying their education. We are all so excited and passionate about this project, and once you've read the delights inside this book, we know you will be too!

Welcome to LETTERS TO AFRICA; you're about to embark on a unique learning experience.

All the best,
The Publishers, SpringbokPress

Dear friend

My name is Jack. I'm 11 years of age (11 and a half really) I'm not all a big fan of sports however I really enjoy Badminton and Netball (I have played a few competitions but lost!) Music is my favourite subject. although I wish I was good at art. You don't want to see me draw; lets just say I'm scary with a paintbrush. How about you, are you interested in art? At least I know one thing, your definitely be better at art than me, no one, and I mean no one is worse than me.

Can you play a musical instrument? I play a cornet, that's a curly trumpet by the way. I also am learning how to play the guitar. What about a favourite food? I love Southern fried chicken! That's chicken basically drowned in spices. Have you a favourite food? Do you only get it on certain occasions like a birthday? What do you do on your birthdays, anything special?

I do wonder what's the most dangerous animal you've "EVER SEEN". Imagine it as your pet, you would be unstoppable!!! Now let's get down to something I would like to know about you! What does every kid love? The answer my friend is games, are there any games that you love? (Because your talking to a hide and seek lover) I bet you and your best friend love to play hide and seek too. Who is your best friend? For all I know your best friend could be your family, I wonder is you have a big family?

I would really like to ask you about your amazing culture, like how you survive for months at a time in the baking heat, It seems so heroic and impossible. hope you enjoyed this letter because I know I'll enjoy hearing from you (^-^).

Yours Sincerely, Jack Sugar, 11

Dear Friend

I have known you for one day. I will write down on this letter my home life.

At home we are seven (7) togethe with my parents nine (9) living in a small house with three (3) rooms a bedroom, sitting room and a kitchen.

Myself and brothers sleep in a kitchen where they use to cook food such as nshima vegetable's. Now my father is trying to build a big house out of the smaller one so that I have my own bedroom together with brother's. Here in zambia we eat nshima with vegetable's such chibwabwa mixed with pounded peanut which we call in our local language (ifisa-shi) and caterpillaries (ifinkubala) while in england which is your country you eat chicken and chips.

I want to improve speaking and writing english so that I study very hard and pass my exams and go to college.

yours faithfully,
SOLOMON KUDALISIOWA.

THE REAL AFRICA

By Mary Hoffman, author of *Amazing Grace*

I have only been to Africa twice. The first time was my trip to The Gambia in 1992, when I was researching for the sequel to my picture book *Amazing Grace* (about a little girl who loves stories). The sequel became *Grace and Family* (Boundless Grace in the US). I was travelling with my illustrator Caroline Binch and she had never been to Africa either.

We visited in December and when we arrived at Banjul airport we were met by a terrifying figure on stilts, which we later learned was called Mama Para – a Christmas character. They were very smiley and energetic but I was very conscious of being a tourist.

I wrote about this trip in *Books for Keeps*:

"The Africa I saw was startling. To Western eyes, homes made up of odd bits and pieces, dirt roads and shoeless children make a strong first impression. It would be dishonest to pretend otherwise in my case. But very quickly your eye begins to take in other things. Palm trees, baobabs, casuarinas, hibiscus, vultures, batik butterflies, and, above all, colours.

Vivid blue skies, purple flowers trailing over our hut-style room at the hotel, cloth of every shade and pattern worn by men and women, particularly spectacular on the women with their matching headcloths twisted into elaborate and becoming styles, piles of pink papaya and red water-melon on our breakfast table... it was like living in a kaleidoscope."

My second trip was to Egypt for a Nile cruise. This was also for work, because I was writing a book called *Seven Wonders of the Ancient World*. Again, I had the feeling that I was being insulated from 'the real Africa' by being a tourist. I loved Egypt and want to go back there one day and show my husband the amazing art in the temples and tombs and the wonderful Museum of Cairo, where the Tutenkamun exhibit nearly stopped my heart. But I know there are other stories about Africa hiding under the surface of what Egypt's visitors get to see.

The British children involved in this project have a real chance to dig deeper and learn about the real Africa. I looked at the things they wrote letters about and wondered what I'd write in my own letter to Africa.

I would write about my school experience. I went to an all-girls school where we had to wear uniform. The best thing was that we had a very well-stocked library where I could hide and read books of myths while bunking off games! I would wonder if the children I was writing to had access to enough books.

I hated PE and all team games but I still enjoyed swimming and walking. I would ask the children in Africa what they liked to do and whether they have the equipment and venues they need.

My life has been revolutionised by technology. Not only do I write quite long novels straight on to the computer; I can start my research there too and stay in touch with friends all over the world through emails, Facebook, Twitter and Skype. Do the African children share these privileges?

A big change that's happened in my life is that my grown-up daughters have at last left home. I miss them but we communicate all the time – I recently received a phone call from one in New York, had a couple of Skype chats with another and all three are soon coming to visit me for my birthday. I live in a big comfortable house with my husband and three cats. I would wonder how much space the children I was writing to had to call their own.

Food is something I enjoy rather too much. I'm a vegetarian and I enjoy cooking as much as I enjoy eating the results. Most of our food is made from scratch and starting with fresh ingredients, and we have a box of organic vegetables delivered every week. I would ask about the food supply in Africa and where the children's families do their shopping.

The answers to these questions will be varied depending on the country, families and individuals concerned, and, similarly, there are a lot of children in the UK who have no access to libraries or technologies in their schools, nowhere quiet to do their homework or just read for fun, little physical exercise and very little fresh fruit and vegetables in their diet. That might surprise the children they are writing to in Africa.

But the world is getting smaller. Britain is not the enclosed little island I grew up in, where I remember seeing my first green pepper and wondering what it was. Would children in Africa guess that the favourite national British dish today is Chicken Tikka Masala? It's wonderful to see the dialogue now possible across continents.

Mary Hoffman
9th April, 2010

HI FRIENDS!

My name is Grace.

Come and meet my friend Jackson - he is a giraffe!

He is going to tell the readers and me all about life in Africa.

Emily Harris, Leyland Methodist School

Abbie Cayton, Woodlea Primary School

© Kate Johnson

© Paula Murray

12

HOME LIFE

Hi Jackson!
I don't like doing chores around the hutch, but my Mum makes me.

How do children in Africa help their parents in the house?

Well Grace, girls help their mothers to collect firewood and water and help milk the goats and cows. The boys start looking after the livestock from an early age.

At the age of six or younger, boys look after baby animals. Boys are given more and more responsibility as they get older, and eventually end up herding the cows at around the age of fourteen!

Dear Friend,
   Hello my name is Alice. I am 10 years old. How old are you? Do you have sisters or brothers? How many? What are your parents like? I live with my Mum, Dad, my sister and my dog called Bruce. I have a garden and a very long drive. I am quite tall I also have long brown hair and hazzel eyes.
   My house is quite big and its very old. What is your house like? Is it old or new? What does it look like? Outside we keep 3 chickens and they lay eggs but not a lot. Do you keep animals at your house? What is your name and what are the names of your animals? Describe yourself and your favourite things? I'd love to know about it?
   At the weekends with my family. Sometimes we play games or go to the cinema. On saterdays my Mum takes me swimming. Do you do things with your family?

                    Yours Sincerely,
                    Alice Singleton

Dear Alice

Hello my name is KAANTII And I am 15 years old. How are you? I have 2 sisters and 3 brothers. My parents like farming and business. We have a garden and livestock. We like drinking milk and growing crop such as tomatoes and maize I am quite tall, I also have long black hair and black eyes. And my favourite thing is like playing football and reading different kind of books.

Our house is quite big and very old made of animal dung and iron sheds. Outside we keep 20 chickens and they lay eggs alot. We keep different kinds of animal in our home like goats, sheeps and cows and bull.

At the weekends I go to the shamba/gardens to help my parents.

I hope to answer my letter from you
Yours Sincerely
KAANTII DICKSON

Dear friend

My name is Ben, I'm 11 years old and have a brother, and a sister. They're both younger than me. Do you have any brothers or, sisters? I have a mum and a dad and we live in England.

In our house we have enough rooms to live in. Is your house made of straw and has one room to live in? Do you ever get cramped in there?

I found out that you cook and wash outside, do you hang your washing up outside? I do. I have always wondered how you make your houses. I can't even put up a tent? Never mind a house.

all the best

Ben Anderton

Dear Ben.

My name is Lilian. I'm 16 years old an I have three brother and three sister. They are younger than me but their is one brother who is bigger than me I have a mum and a dad and we were living together in Kenya. In our home we have many neibours and they help us.

We have enough room in our house and also for people who came to visite us.

In our house we have toiles in it and a kichen, bafe and also such kind of things.

We have all kind of sport. I like football and netball. Even I, support man united. They are good players. We have deffierent kind of animals in our home those are dogs, cats hens and cocks and cows, sheeps, and goat. I love them.

We remove the wool of a sheep and make cloths for peoples.

All the best from
Lilian.

Dear Kenyan friend,
My name is Elsa. Whats your name?
I am 10 years old. I like animals especially
horses. I read lots of books!

My family has only 3 members in it including
my Mum, my Dad and me. well my cats are
included so that makes 5. I live in a
small village in a bungalow, its a house
with no stairs. There is a field near my garden
with sheep and cows and 2 horses and a
donkey that wakes me up at 6.00 in the
morning.

Yours sincerly
Elsa.

Dear Elga....

my name is Solonka. I am a 15 year old boy. I like animals cows, goats and sheeps. Every saturday morning i go to see animals.

i go to to enkajinaibor primary I like Learning and reading. do you read?

My family have only 6 members and 110 animals like pigs.

my mum is called rebeka and my Dad is called Lasarous also we have

a grand father and a grand mother they like us and they tell us stories about the past.

our houses are made by mud and grass. How do yours? In our home we eat many foods like meats ugali and porrehge.

In the morning we have cock tell us it is morning. I have a small dog called papilo and I like Him. Every night it bark to tell us their is a thief near our home.

I would like to see you my friend

Yours Loving
Solonka.

Hi,

My name is Emma Rowley. I live in England, in a town called Oswaldtwistle. I am tall, with light brown hair, and Hazel eyes. I wear glasses. I am a girl, and go to Hippings Methodist school.

Anyway, thats enough about me, I want to know about you. What do you do for fun? Do you help around the house? I do, I clean and cook, my mum is always grateful.

How many rooms are in your house? What are they like? I have nine rooms in my house, including the cellar. What is your favourite room in your house? Mine is the kitchen (I love cooking).

I have two brothers called Brandon and Gareth, (they really annoy me). Do you have any brothers or sisters? What are their names?

I live with my mum, (Catriona) and my brothers. My Dad is called Darren he was born in South Africa. My other family live miles away, or in a different country.

I am eleven years old, how old are you? What is your name?

From Your new friend Emma Rowley ☆

My guinea pig

KABWE
ZAMBIA

Hi   friend

My name is Joseph Mutale, am a zambia
citizen age 14 years old. I live in katondo
and i go to the school called katondo upper
basic school, where i live is not far from
school. My hobbies are drawing and playing
soccer, i love drawing because am good at
drawing.

The funniest thing is that i go school.
When i grow up i want to become a desiner
Engineer.

The saddest thing that has happened to
me is that my parents are dead and i have no
support, My Mother died in 2006 when i was
at the age of 10 year. I live with my Grandma.

My favourite room is My bed room.

My favourite colour is yellow
but my bed room is not yellow
I would like to know more
about your country.

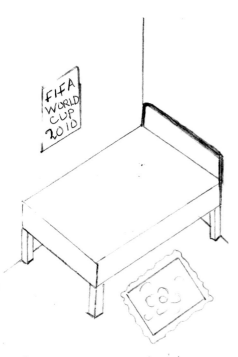

FIFA
WORLD
CUP
2010

It looks like this

YOUR FRIEND

JOSEPH MUTALE

Dear Friend,

My name is Sammy Jo, I am 11 years old, I have blonde hair, which is long and blue eyes.

I live on a dairy cattle farm with my Dad, Mom and 23 year old Sister. I also have a 26 year old brother who is married and doesn't live with us. Do you have any brothers or sisters?

I have one border collie sheepdog called Tilly and one black and white cat called Pebbles.

I enjoy living on a farm. Do you live on a farm? We have 60 cows and they are friesan Holsteins.

At home I ride my bike, go on my trampoline and go on my two swings. What do you enjoy doing at home?

My house is an old farmhouse made of stone. I live by a stream with a woods on the otherside which I play in. What is your house like?

Yours Sincerely

Sammy Jo Milner

Dear friend Sammy

My name is Philp Kilelo Parut I am 16 year old.

I live on a cattle farm with my Dad, mum and 23 year old

sister. I have also a 12 year old Brother who is Martine

My Father have cows sheeps and goats he Give me 20 cows

5 Sheeps and 7 Goats

I have 20 Dogs all of them have Names an old dog called

Bosko a young one called Kuchi I would like to see yours my

friend

In my family are many People like father, mother, granfather,

granmother, and children We're living in Place Called Emesera

Philip Kilel
Parut

IT'S NOT LIKE WHERE I'M FROM

By Victoria Todd

Will jumped as he heard the key crunch in the lock. He checked his watch; it was quarter past ten. His mum's voice floated down the hall to him; followed by a very quiet voice he had never heard before, saying, 'It's not like where I'm from...'

'Will! What on earth are you still doing up?' Will put on his best-behaved smile as his mum walked in, followed by a scared-looking girl. 'I told you that you could meet Chanya in the morning.'

'Sorry, Mum,' Will said, still smiling, 'I couldn't wait. Al's in bed, but I couldn't sleep, I was too excited. Hello.' Will turned to Chanya, who was looking at him without blinking. 'I'm Will. What do you think of England so far?'

Chanya mumbled something, and Will had to ask her to repeat herself.
'I said, it's not like this where I come from,' she whispered.

'I'll tell you what, seeing as though you're both up, why don't we have some hot chocolate before bed?' Will's mum said, and disappeared into the kitchen.

'What's so different about your home, then?' Will asked curiously. Chanya sat silently for so long on the Walker's sofa that Will thought she wasn't going to answer. He was racking his brains for something to say when she suddenly spoke.

'My house is much smaller,' Chanya said. 'It's very dark, and we don't spend much time in there. We spend most of our time outside, looking after the animals. I'm in charge of the goats,' she said, looking proud. 'I was only in charge of the kids until last year, but now me and my brothers look after the big goats as well!'

'Wow,' Will marvelled. 'I've been asking Mum for a dog for ages, and she doesn't think I can look after it! Wait 'til I tell Mum that!'

'Tell me what, Will?' his mum said as she walked through, carrying two mugs of hot chocolate. She gave one to Chanya and one to Will.

'Tell her, Chanya,' Will said, but Chanya had gone shy again and drank her hot chocolate so she did not have to answer.

'Chanya looks after a whole load of goats, Mum,' Will said. 'And they're very valuable, aren't they, Chanya?' Chanya nodded, still drinking. 'Wow, Chanya, I bet you'd find it really easy to look after one little dog, wouldn't you, if you're trusted with all the goats?' Chanya flashed a grin, suddenly understanding.

'Yes, I bet dogs are much less trouble than goats, and just one would be very easy,' she said, innocently. Will smirked at his mum.

'Will, I'm gone for two minutes and you've already got her on your side? I've told you before; we'll see,' Will's mum said, shaking her head. 'I've made you a bed up in the spare room, Chanya, but if you don't want to be on your own, Will can have his sleeping bag on the floor.' Chanya nodded. 'All right,' Will's mum said. 'But don't be up all night talking. Your dad's going to pick you up for school in the morning; I'm picking Elliot up from the airport. Goodnight, guys.' Will's mum picked up the empty mugs and took them to the kitchen.

Later on, Chanya was tucked up in bed, and Will was in his sleeping bag on the floor. The light was switched off, but they had been talking for over an hour. Will was eating biscuits, and Chanya was munching on a chocolate bar that Will had smuggled out of the kitchen on their way up to bed. 'Where's your dad then?' Chanya asked, through a mouthful of chocolate. 'And who's Elliot?'

Will could see that it was already time for the long-winded explanation of his family. 'Elliot's my stepdad. He's away at a conference, but he'll be back tomorrow so you'll get to meet him. He's loads of fun, for an adult. He's Al's dad. That's Alistair, my half-brother. My dad lives at the other side of town, with my stepmum, Annie. I think we might visit them while you're over here. I have two stepsisters there, Karen and Michelle. They're nice but they're older than me. Karen's seventeen and Michelle's twenty, so they don't do much with me. Alistair's only seven, so he likes to play with me, but he's so babyish. I bet your family wouldn't even let him look after the kid goats.'

Chanya was quiet, and Will wondered if he had confused her with all his different relatives. Sometimes he confused himself.

'It's not like that where I'm from, but it's not too different,' Chanya said. 'My dad has two wives after my mum, but Maasai women – like my mum – are only allowed one husband. Men can have as many wives as they can take care of.'

Will sat up in the dark, interested. 'So do you have lots of brothers and sisters, then?'
'Yes,' Chanya said longingly. 'My mum has a boy and two other girls, and Dad's other wives have a boy each. We all look after each other though, it's lots of fun. And we're all nearly the same age, so we're in the same class at school, except for my oldest brother, Amari; he's fifteen. He was initiated last year, so he's going to be a warrior now.'

'A warrior?' Will asked, astounded.

'Yeah, he's growing his hair long, and he wears the red wrap, and carries a spear and thinks he's brilliant,' Chanya said, sounding fed up. 'He used to be loads of fun, but now he's an adult he just thinks he's the most important, especially because he's a warrior, not at school like us kids.'

'Wow, I can't wait to meet them,' Will said, snuggling back down in his sleeping bag.

'It's all the elders' fault, for letting him be initiated so young,' Chanya said grumpily.

'Who are the elders?' Will asked, his eyes closing of their own accord.

'They're the older men. They used to be warriors but now they're in charge of the whole village,' Chanya replied sleepily. 'They don't have much to do with me yet, I don't think they're interested in a lost kid like me.'

'Lost?' Will yawned.

'Yes, it's what they call children who go to school. I probably won't be initiated and I won't get to do all the traditional rituals but at least the elders won't choose a husband for me.' Chanya's voice was quiet, and Will could barely hear her as he dropped off to sleep.

'I'm looking forward to doing the exchange back to your place, Chanya,' he said sleepily. 'Warriors and elders and animals; it's not like where I come from. I can't wait.'

GOING TO SCHOOL

In the U.K. children go to school when they are four, and leave when they are sixteen.

Many children don't like going to school very much!

They learn subjects such as History, Literacy, Numeracy and Science.

All Maasai children speak Maa as their first language, Swahili as their second language and English as their third language. Lessons are taught in Swahili and English.

In Zambia, children often don't start school until they are seven or eight. They are grouped into grades by their ability rather than age.

They will only go up to the next grade when they are ready, so people can still be at school when they are twenty.

Dear friend in africa,

hi my name is Thomas and I am going to tell you about my life in england. I know that it is very hard for you over in africa, so I hope that this letter will cheer you up.

My day at school is normally crammed with tests and practises. Every day we do Maths and english and a range of other subjects which I don't like. Don't tell any one but secretly I love school!

When I was in year five we made musical instruments out of various materials such as wood elastic bands and paint. I made a kind of 4 way guitar it looked good at the start (but in the end it fell apart.)

Eneogh about me what about you? do you enjoy school? do you ever play games at school? do you have pens at school? do you get animals at school?

from Thomas

Dear Thomas

Hello! My name is Samuel, I am 15.

I am a stardard eight pupil from Enhii primary school. I knows it is very hard for us to meet each other but we can commicate through this proces, I am a cardidate of this year 2010, so I am waiting for my Exams. English same to you is my best subject but also i can do very nice in scence and maths, those are my best subject that I usualy paform in the class,

In our country kenya we have a very beutuful enuaroment, in our natinal park We have many wild animal bike bion, elephant, hippo, zebra, many bard and also fishes are pound in Lakes and rivers, we usualy visit to our game parks, to enjoy how beutuful our country kenya is;

in our school we have about eleven teacher and also three hundred and ninety pupils our school is made of stones and also timber.

In our school we have games and sports, I usually peform in volley ball; in English premier League I usually supoul chelsea. What abovo you?

Samuel Kuyan

Hi Kenya Friend,

Hi I am Jonathan George Taylor, I am Ten years old, and I go to Ribby with wrea CE Primary School.

I start my day by travelling to school in a shiny silver car. How do you get to school?

My school is very small, it only holds one hundred and twenty two pupils! It's really small! How big is your school? Our school was founded an extremely long time ago by a man called James Thisthleton. He gave us some money to found our wonderful school almost 400 years ago in 1693!

And now on to a really good part, our school LUNCHES! They are yummy! We have to go to lunch at 12:00 - 1:00.

Next onto our lessons, we have four lessons per day. We have Maths in the morning, English in the morning, and two other lessons in the afternoon. How many lessons do you have? Do you have a playground? We have computers which are clever electrical devices, calculators for maths, And most certainly more!

I am very thankful for you reading my letter!

I look forward to hearing from you!

From

Jonathan Taylor

Dear JONATHAN GEORGIK TAYLOR

I am seventeen years old, and I go to ENKILL primary school. I have black and white eyes and black hair. I have a mother and father / also have one sister and finally / have a black tan dog (called simba. / am from Rift valley which is a central part of Kenya.

I starts my day by travelling to school by foot. In our school We have eight teachers. The name of our headteacher is Mr. Rafael teacheri. My school is very small compared to those in Kenya its only with four hundred pupils. Our school was started by another European who was constructing the pipeline which transports water from mt Kilimanjaro the highest mountain in Africa to Nairobi. it was started in 1948 with fourty two pupils.

In our school we have only six lessons. English in the morning and maths and other lessons in afternoon. Do you have a Kiswahili lesson in your school? We have black boards to write on and the teacher use what we call chalk we also have a very large playground but we don't have computers in our school since it in a very poor place.

I am looking foward to
hearing from you!
from

LEYIAN NG'ASHAR

Dear Friend,

Hello my name is Ellie. What is your name?
My favourite subjects in school are Art, and literacy.
What is your favourite hobby in school?
Could you tell me about your self and what you like
to do in school. We go on many School trips. Do you go on
many school trips?

We have Blue, Black and grey uniform, do you have coloured
uniform? Could you tell me what colour uniform
you have please?
We have wooden and metal tables, all separated. Our walls
are decorated in Maths and literacy things.
If you have decorated walls? could you tell me about them?

Yours ~~Sincerely~~ Sincerely
Ellie. Age 10.

Dear friend

HA! My name is Joan Chuuu. I was born on 1st February 1995 at Kabwe General hospital in Kabwe I started school at a tender age of 6 at Katondo Basic. Since I stay near to the school I just walk about 15 minutes. This time am doing my Grade nine at K.T Basic. We are four in my family two girls and two boys. I am the second born first born is a boy doing his Grade eleven at highridge high school I stay with my mum and Grandmother We live in a house which is made up of bricks and has my mum works every month she get the salarie of K200000 we are not rich or poor but we are on between My best subject that I like mostly or my favourite subjects is Mathematics so that has I complete my education I would like to be an accountant. My hobbies are playing netball, dancing and cooking but remember our traditional food is nshima

Your Friend
Joan

Dear child

Hi my name Is Isabel, I am 8 years old and I live in the UK. I live in a house with my mum, Dad and two kitten's India and Asia there both Evil!!!!!! (and cute!)

My school is called Woodlea Junior school. I am in class LR my best buddies are Lydia, Alisha and Me. I go to school 6 day's a week and I only get two days of, (Sooo not Fair!) Are school uniform is sooo old Fashioned it's a white t-shirt with a horrible jumper and a skirt or pants and socks and a pair of shoes. I also love swimming it's so much Fun.

How much electricity do you have?
Do you like it in kenya?

Isabel

dear friend I Sabel

my Name is susan kiike. I am 13 Year Old   and I Live in Kenya.
I Live in a house with my mother, father, dads and brothers
two goat and five cattles.
my Schools is called. ENkaJi_Naibor I am in class 7. my best
buddies are Nchaa and Nkaitai.
I go to Shcol 5 days Per weeks are school uniform is blue dress
and Yellow Collar, blue Jumper and white socks, black Shoes
I also love Planting brees in our home Compound. I have
elebriesety I am short of food. I enjoy it in kenya.

Your faith fully

SUSAN KIIKE

Dear, Friend, :)

I am a 10 year old girl called Caitlin, I absolutely love to read books, my two favourites are The night of the unicorn and Black beauty. Do you read? If you do, what is your favourite book? I also like writing Stories of my own I try my best to make them good. Do you write your own stories? If you don't why don't you give it a go if you can?

I hear that you play mancala in your country, I would like to know how to play it, If you don't mind could you tell me how? Also, I am very good at football.

Me and my brother go to a great primary school called Farington. They teach us things that are very interesting, at the moment we are learning about plants because our topic is Earth keepers and that's why we are learning about the amazing things on Earth. At school my favourite lesson is Maths because of all the thinking. What is your favourite lesson if you go to school> I also have two best friends called Danielle and Jayden. Do you have any friends?

Yours sincerely,
Caitlin :)

Dear Caitlin,

How are you my friend? My name is Keteko Isaiah. I am fourteen years old. I am a boy. I am interested in reading and studing books. One of my interest story is the story of The Berkut. I do also writing and discussing stories with my friends. Thank you my friend, you can read the fun game below:

A FUN GAME   Ding / Leding — Conversation between them

Ding: What is your name?
Leding: I wish I knew.
Ding: If we take you to Jail?
Leding: Then I will wail.

This is just fun game we play with my friends. We Keep on discussing stories and making fun games like the one I tell you before. Oh! my friend I don't understand what's mancala! Please tell me on your next letter.

Me and my sisters go to Enkii Primary school. It is located in Loitokitok district in Kenya. They teach us many subject. They include Science, Maths, Social studies and others like English, Kiswahili and Christian Religious Education.

My favourite Lessons is on English times and Maths. But the best is Maths. I also have friends namely Mutero and John.

Thank Advance
Yours faithfull
Keteko.

KIANO'S CHOICE

By Victoria Todd

On a hot sunny morning, on the first day back at school, the children of class 6T walked into their classroom to find a new pupil sat nervously at a desk. He had greyish black hair, big brown eyes and an enormous nose, and he was twiddling his hooves uncomfortably. Dalila was the first to speak. She walked up to the desk and looked him over.

'Hello. My name's Dalila,' she said, smiling at him, 'and I'm a girl. Who are you?' The new pupil shuffled in his seat and would not look at Dalila.

'I'm Kiano,' he replied, in such a quiet voice that Dalila had to lean in to hear him. 'And I'm a donkey.' Dalila nodded wisely and sat down next to him at the wooden desk. Encouraged by Dalila's attitude, the other children came in and crowded around him curiously.

'Have you just moved here?' Peter asked, perching on the edge of the desk. Kiano nodded.

'Yes, my mum and dad moved here a week ago,' Kiano said. 'I like it here, but I miss my old home. There were lots of donkeys there.'

Peter started to reply, but Gladys had spotted the teacher coming, so all of the students ran to their seats and tried to look as if they had been behaving.

The children of class 6T felt like they had never had a longer morning. They had to sit through double maths, which Kiano was very good at, and English, which he was not. His pencil kept slipping through his hooves and falling to the floor, which made him go hot with embarrassment. He fumbled with it under his desk and it kept slipping out of his grasp, until the teacher cleared his throat crossly. Dalila quickly leant over and picked the pencil up for him.

Kiano smiled at her in relief, and a breeze blew through the window frame, cooling him down. His eyes strayed out into the yard that was bright with sunshine, and his heart jumped. It must be nearly break time!

Ten minutes and two pencil-catchings from Dalila later, Kiano saw the little children from classes 1J and 2L running out into the yard. He looked hopefully up at the teacher, and was so excited he dropped his pencil again. The teacher looked at the pencil, then at Kiano. He sighed.

'Go on then, class,' the teacher said, still looking at Kiano. 'And I hope you'll concentrate harder after break, young man. Erm… young donkey.' Kiano nodded and pelted out of the classroom on all fours. He stood up in the dusty playground, his eyes bright, waiting for the others to catch up to him. Dalila reached him first.

'You can run really fast!' Dalila said, catching her breath. Kiano looked down modestly as the rest of the class caught up.

'I like playing sport, it's my favourite thing to do,' Kiano said shyly.

'What about maths?' Matu asked. 'You were rubbish at English, but you were really good at maths.'

'Matu!' Dalila said, shocked. Kiano went hot again, but he shook his head.

'It's OK Dalila, I'm not very good at English,' Kiano said. 'In my old school we didn't have pencils and paper; we had chalk and a slate board. The chalk was much thicker than a pencil and I could hold it easier. And slate is harder to rip than paper, too!'

Matu and Dalila laughed. Peter kicked a football towards them, and when Kiano returned the ball back across the pitch, the children playing cheered.

'Do you like school, Kiano?' Dalila asked her new friend, curiously. Kiano looked sad.

'Yes, I love learning new things,' he said, looking down at the ground. 'But my mum and dad don't want me to stay at school. They said it's up to me, but they would prefer it if I was a traditional donkey, like my big brother Runo. He's working really hard at the moment. He gets loads of responsibility, like he gets to go to the market and carry all the loads. It looks like fun, but I'm not allowed to go. I've been with him to get the water from the well though; that was hard work, so I'm glad I don't have to do that. My sister Aluna went to school and she ended up leaving us to go and live with her friends who had been to school with her. She said I could live with them if I stay at school, but I don't know. She's a teacher now. I'd love to do that. But I don't want to leave home.'

'I know how you feel,' Dalila said kindly. 'My mum and dad want me to come to school, they want me to learn things and get a good job, but Matu's family don't want him to be here, do they, Matu?'

Matu nodded. 'I chose to come to school anyway, and they don't like it much. They say I'm 'lost', because I don't spend all my time at home like my brothers. But I like it here.' Matu grinned. 'Most of the time, anyway. And my brothers are married now, with their own families.'

Dalila wrinkled her nose. 'I'd hate to get married so young. That's why I'm glad my mum and dad send me here. I don't have to get married for years yet!'

Kiano laughed. 'My brother didn't want to get married young either, but he did, and he says it's brilliant. Aluna doesn't believe him, but she likes looking after his two foals. So do I, they're really cute. But I don't want any of my own!'

'What, ever?' asked Dalila, her eyes widening.

'Well maybe some day,' he said. 'But not for a long, long time! I want to travel the world and teach other people and learn about everything!'

'Seems like you've made your mind up, then,' Dalila laughed. 'You must want to stay at school!'

Kiano looked thoughtful. 'Yes,' he said. 'I suppose I do.'

He stood quietly for a moment, thinking about growing up and teaching people like his big sister did. He smiled, and opened his mouth to speak when Peter's football hit him in the leg. Dalila chased after it, and Kiano followed her towards the football pitch.

'Kiano,' a voice said. Kiano turned around to see the teacher walking towards him. He bent his head, embarrassed.

'I'm glad you're making friends. I'm sorry I was hard on you in class, but the other children were getting silly. I'm very impressed with your maths skills, and don't worry about English. I heard what you said to Dalila about using not using pencils and paper at your old school; we'll get you some chalk and slate. It might be hard work at first, but I promise it will be worthwhile.' The teacher smiled at Kiano. 'Now go off and play football!'

Kiano trotted towards the football pitch. He had not had chance to say it out loud, but thought it over to himself instead: *With friends like Dalila, Matu and Peter, and a future like Aluna's, I think I'm going to like it here.*

ANIMALS

Cows are the most important animal to the Maasai in Kenya, and can only be owned by men.

Owning cattle is highly respected as it shows how wealthy a Maasai man is.

The Maasai people have great respect for all animals, and they call wild animals their brothers.

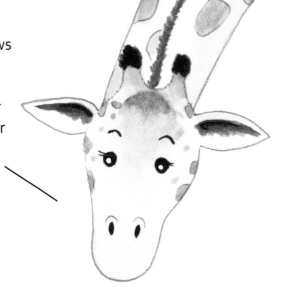

In the U.K. many households have pets such as dogs, cats or guinea pigs. (Like me!)

We see cows and goats in fields in the countryside.

We can't see big animals like you, Jackson, unless we go to a zoo!

Dear friend,

My name is Amber Metherell. I am 10 years of age. I have long, straight, dark blonde hair and brown eyes. I have a female tabby cat named Kanga. Do you have any pets? I would love to have a pet snake. It would be cool! Animals running free round here are mainly rabbits, mice, gray squirrels, a range of insects, small spiders and sometimes rats.

What kind of animals roam free near you? We have to go to zoos and wild-life parks to see the animals you see most of the time. My favourite animals are proberbly tigers, cheetahs and snakes. But, then, I hardly ever see any! What are your favourite animals? Sometimes I wish I could see more of these endangered species before they are wiped out. I mean, it would seem hilairious to us to see a tiger parading accross the Green! The scariest animal I have ever seen is a Goliath Bird-eating Spider. What is the scariest animal for you? Thankyou for taking the time to read my letter. I hope to hear from you soon!

from, Amber Metherell

Dear friend. AMBER:

my name is Parmuya NOAH, I am 13 years old. I am in class Seven, I live in a village called esambu. my School name is eNkaji Naibor I love it very much. I started being in this school in the year of 2004.

In our village we have caws and goats. We herd our cow's in the forest every day for the cow to produce more milk When they eat alot of pasture they will produce more meat then the other day when they don't eat pasture.

Your Sincerly Parmuya

Thank you!

Dear Kenya friend

My name is Toby Gilmore. I am ten years old.
I like German shepherd dogs, Scuba diving, snorkerling and looking at fish. I do not like cats, mushrooms, goats, milk, baboons, The one show and girls from ribby with wrea.

I am going to get a German shepherd dog which is related to the wolf and it looks like a wolf exsept it's fur is black and ginger and I am getting it in two weeks.

These are the animals that I see sometimes, dogs, cats, squirrles, foxes and phesrants. To see some animals you see we have to go to a zoo.

My favourite animal is a dog what is your favourite animal?

My least favourite is a baboon.

It would be nice to hear from you again.
From
Toby Gilmore.

my Dear Toby Gilmoe. I am → fourteen years old I have
two sister and a mum and Dad. I go to Enkaji Naibor school.
My eyes are black in and white outside.

ON Kenya we have more Animals for example is Cheetar Lion Gazells
goat Cow giraffe Elephant, monkey. The most Problem of these Animals is when you
Plant thing like tomatoes onion maize and beens. those Animal they
Con Come to your gorden to eat Something which you have Planted.

~Your friend
KASyoki muTinda
Thank you.

Our Traditional hut

ELEPHANT

Dear children,
Hi, my name is Jessica and I am eleven years old I have brown hair that only just ties up in a bobble and my eyes are blue. My mum is called Michelle and her friend is called Laura who lives with me. Now I've told something about myself I would like to ask you a few questions. whats your worst and favourite animal in africa? My favourite animal is the monkey but my worst is a snake. I like monkeys because they swing from very high trees therefore I hate snakes because they slither and I feel like they would bite me.

If you was an inventer what three animals would you mix to make a new animal? I would mix an elephant, giraffe and a kangaroo. I would call it a kangaffphant. It would have a elephants face and ears, a giraffes neck and legs, last but not least a kangaroos body and pouch.

　　　　　Thank you for
　　　　reading my
　　　　letter
　　　　　Jessica Kelly

Dear Jessica

+ Hi. My name is Jane and I am Seventeen years old. I have two sisters and three brothers. My mum is called Elizabeth. She work at the place of shoping center. My father is called Joel

We live in a climate of many different changes. Sometime it is very hot, cool and wet.

In my country Kenya they are many animals elephants, giraffe and Hippo and. Mostly I like zebra because it has two colours which I like very much and enjoy.

Yours Sincely
Jane Kaperik

Zebura

Hi, my name is Olivia Schofield and I am 10 years old, how old are you? I have brown hair, green eyes and I am tall.

What is your favourite animal? Mine is a Elephant because I think they are really cute. I have no pet animals because my dad is allergic to them. Would you like a pet, and what would it be?

What animal scares you the most, and why? The animal that scares me is a cockroach because when I was on holiday in Spain, I was in bed when I saw a cockroach crawling across the floor (I thought it was a leaf at first then it moved! What animal is most common in Africa?

I have never had a pen pal, but I have always wanted one, I hope you can be my pen pal forever. I forgot to ask you before, what is your name?

Olivia

Dear Olivia

Hey, my name is Joyce Shiluni and I am 13 years old, I live in Kimana which is near Loitokitok. my house is quite small but not so small. My home is so good because i have one dad, one mum, two sisters and three brothers.

I like so many animals like cows, sheep and goats. My favourite Animal is a cow. because a cow gives as milk, skin, and meat.

The animal which scares me the most, is a bee because it gives us honey.

I have never had a Pen Pal, but i have always wanted one, I hope that now you are my Pen Pal.

From Joyce Shiluni

Dear Friend,

My name is Zoe. I am 10 years old and I live in New Longton. I used to have a pecock, well it was't relly mine but I called it mine. It was a wild pecock but it always came in my back garden. We fed it and keeped it clean but one day someone in the avenu called the R.S.P.C.A. and Ashly (that was his name) got taken away to be put in a cage. He never came back. Since Ashly has been gone we have had about 1 thousend fish. We've got 25 now. I have one and my sister emma has the other 24. I've told my mum and dad how much I would love to have a snake as a pet but emma is scard of them. She thinks that they are so horible and slimy but I think its cute the way they stick out there tongue and smell the air. Do you like snakes? If you do wich is your fave? Mine's a corn snake.

I hope to hear the ansers from you soon
Yours Sincerly
Zoe

Dear Zoe

I am Muntees Ketukei, I am 13 years old I am a boy.

I go to school at Enkaji naibor primary school, I like school very much. Our school is near two small rocky hills. it is a beatiful school.

We have a few animals that is Cows, goat and sheeps, They go for grazing and come back home in the evening. We benefit atot from this animals. a cow give us milk, a goat give us meat and sheep give us wool and fat.

I look after our animals durings weekends, and my parents do milking cows in the morning and evening. I like milk as my favourite food.

Thank you my dear friend and
God bless you so much

Yours Sincerely.
Muntees Ketukei.

©Gemma Nolan

WHY DO MONKEYS LIVE UP TREES?

by Dorothy Massey

Old Bushcat was hungry;
she'd hunted all day.
So under the shade
of a tree she did lay.

She was tired and weary,
Needing badly to rest,
but the fleas started biting
and being a pest.

The beautiful sunset
she looked up to see -
caught sight of a monkey,
above, in the tree.

"Oh monkey, please help me!
Get rid of these fleas.
They're really a nuisance.
Get them off me, please!"

Monkey swung down,
from his branch in the tree
and one at a time
he picked off each flea.

Bushcat was happy
and fell fast asleep.
With no fleas to annoy her;
her slumber was deep.

Now, Monkey was naughty
by nature, you see.
He tied Bushcat's tail to
a branch of the tree.

Bushcat was mad when
she woke up and found
her beautiful tail
to a tree had been bound.

She twisted like this
and she twisted like that,
but twisting's no use
to a poor, tree-bound cat.

When darkness was falling,
And falling quite fast,
Bushcat spied a snail,
trying to slink past.

"Snail!" Bushcat shouted,
"Oh Snail, hear my plea,
untie my poor tail,
which is bound to this tree."

"No way!" said the snail,
"You will eat me, I fear,
if I untie your tail
and you're awfully near."

"No, I won't," said Bushcat.
"I will solemnly vow
that I won't eat you, Snail,
if you untie me now."

Snail untied Bushcat,
and he went on his way.
Bushcat said to himself,
"That bad monkey will pay."

"I will get my own back
On that monkey, I swear.
I've a trick of my own,
which will give him a scare."

She instructed her friends
to pretend she was dead.
Her friends thought it strange,
but they did as she said.

When five days had passed,
Bushcat lay on the ground,
She lay still as a stone
while her friends danced around.

When Monkey came near,
Bushcat jumped up with glee.
The terrified Monkey,
Sprang into a tree.

And that is why Monkey,
won't stay on the ground.
He'll be up in the tree,
in case Bushcat's around.

SPORTS AND GAMES

My little legs aren't very good for playing sports, Jackson, but I love playing games!

What games do you see children playing in Africa?

Children in Zambia play a game called bacola. A bottle or container is placed on top of a mound of earth or sand.

Members of each team take turns to throw a ball with the aim of knocking over the bottle. When someone succeeds, the ball is passed from person to person until the winning team manages to get the ball into a circle round the cone.

Hello,

My name is Amy, I am 11 years old. I live in Wrea Green. Wrea Green is a little village near Preston. I am going to talk to you about sport we do here in England. I am very sporty. I do swimming, football, athletics, netball, cricket and tennis. What sport do you do? I love anything to do with running or even walking. I have just got a new dog called Bobby and I take him for walks which he likes.

Do you have any funny sport memories, because I do and here it is: I was playing tag rugby and we were kicking the ball over a football goal and when it was my turn I went to kick the ball, I took a run up and missed the ball completely and fell over "Splat!" Straight into the mud!!

I hope you can respond soon. Yours sincerely,

Amy Croasdale

Dear Friend Amy

I am SEMPETU I am 11 years old. I live in a village called Egambu in our village we have many Couls many Guats and we have a dog. We see many lions.

in our house we have one brother three sisters and my father.

my father have very big Garden we plant tomatos

me I play football in our school i support Chelsea.

I draw my house

Sempetu

I like it

Hi,

My name is Andrew, I am 10 years old.
I have two sisters and one brother, and a Mum and
Dad.

My favourite game is golf and football, in golf
you use clubs (sticks with a peice of wood on the end)
then you hit it with a ball and try to get it in
a tiny hole. You know what football is! What
sports do you play? How do you play then?
Are they good? It's good for Africa that your
country has the world cup! The sports I
don't like are croqeat and rugby which I don't
know alot about.

Well thats all I have to say for now.
Please write back! I hope you can tell me about
yourself!

from
Andrew M.

Hy, Andy! Dear Andrew

My name is Felix .M. Musikeri, I am 15 years old. I am in the seventh grade in Enkii primary School in Loitoktok. Loitoktok is the South part of Kenya.

I have four Sister and two brothers, and a mum but no father.

My nick name is Fely.

My favourite game is football and valleyball. in football, The ball is put on the centre of the field. After the whistle, One of the team Starts the ball, And tries to score the goal.

And volley ball you hit it on you hands and try to keep it in the other side of the net, when it fall down that is a score for you. I like it So much.

Our Country "KENYA" is leading now in Africa Cup of nation in football. I don't know how to play Rugby ball".

from
FELix .M. Musikeri

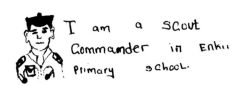 I am a Scout Commander in Enkii primary school.

Dear Kenyan friend

My name is Emily. I am 9 years old. I live in Preston in England. I live with my mum and dad.
I have lots of friends at school. We like dancing. We do street dance, Ballet, Tap, Hip hop and lots of lifts. One day we did a lift and I fell on my bum (My friend Katie dropped me.)
The other sports we do are Dodgeball, Football, running and rounders. The aim of rounders is to hit the ball and run round 4 posts before the ball gets frown and caught 4 times. If you beat the ball your team gets a point. What sports and games do you play in Kenya? I would realy like to know. There is one game that is extremely populer wich is Tig. Do you play Tig? If not its ok.

Hope you write back. Love Emily

This is me.

Dear EMILY

Hello my name is Samuel Mwangai. I am
16 years old. I am in Standard eight in Enkii
primary school. I live in Loitoktok in Kenya.
The subject i like most is Kiswahili and English.

Our teacher normally teach us about England
how it is beautiful in Kenya. At school i normally
Papicipate in two clubs scout club and Environmental
Club. in Premier league I usually support Chelsea.
in Kenya we normally play a game known us
Hind and Sick in England do you know that game?
There is also another game in kenya known us

one touch. it is to use only one ball and four goal
Post

Thankyou for your very interesting letter.

Samuel

Dear friend

My name is Sonia and I am 10 years old.

My favourite game is monopoly. It is a game where the winner is the one with the most money. This game can take a very long time to finish. My favourite sport is netball. The aim of the game is to score as many goals as possible. I am quite good at aiming and throwing at the goal net. The most common sport in my class is football. I also like football so I would teach football. I admire Lionel Messi. A football player from Barcelona. The funniest thing that has happened to me whilst playing sport, is when I was winning a race until my hairband fell out. I turned back to pick it up. When it was in my hair I had lost the race!

Thank-you for reading and I hope to hear from you.

Yours sincierly Sonia

Dear friend

My name is Benson Mwape. I'm 14 years old and am doing my grade 7 at Twafwane Community school. Am the third born in the family of six.

I like watching movies, playing soccer and having fun with friends. I also like going hunting in the bush with my friends and swimming in rivers.

I am a Liverpool supporter "Never walk alone". It's very nice to hear from you!

Are you coming for the world cup games?

Yours
Benson!

Hi whoever is reading this,

I'm Jordan. I'm in Lancashire in England and I'm an 11 year old girl. How old are you? I was born in Scotland.

What sort of sports do you have in Zambia We have tennis, netball, football and a few more I was also wondering is you have a favorite sports person? I don't have a favorite sports person because I don't watch sports. What is your favorite game?

The funniest thing happened to me last summer, I was playing the goal keeper in a game of football and I stopped the ball, not with my hands, not with my feet, but with my face! I thought my nose was going to start bleeding, (lukily it didn't)

I really hope you liked my letter and I can't wait to hear yours. I hope you have a good day and lots of fun.

Yours Faithfully Jordan Hindle.

Dear friend,

I hope and trust all with you is fine and the family are in good health. I've never had a friend from overseas. I am a zambian girl of 15 years old and go to school in Kabwe

I'm a nsolo player a traditional game in zambia played by two players

nsolo is done either on ground or carved wood. This is the way nsolo looks like

Player one (1)

these belong to player(1)two

→ holes

→ player(2) two

Player two (2)

you put two (2) stones in each hole for me to teach other children nsolo I would have to demonstrate

My favourite sports person is Esther phiri a lady boxer. She is the first lady boxer in zambia who has brought honeur to the country. Esther phiri has won both in Africa and overseas.

Yours Sincerely
Innely C maambo

LET'S PLAY!

by Dorothy Massey

Fostina waited and waited at the playing field, but there was still no sign of her best friend, Millika. *I wonder what's wrong?* she thought. Millika never misses Sport in Action.

"Hey, Fostina! Are you coming to play netball or not?" shouted Grace.

"I'm coming!" Fostina tore across the playing field to join the older girls. Grace handed Fostina a tabard. She pulled it over her head and was soon warming up. Fostina watched one of the younger children holding the netball high above her head, running in zigzags around the field. A large group of even younger ones chased the girl, trying to get the ball from her. They're going to ruin the netball game, thought Fostina. I wish Millika was here. She'd keep them amused.

"Were you waiting for someone?" asked Grace.

"Yes. Millika," said Fostina. "She said she'd be here."

"Oh! Millika stayed back to do extra English," Grace told her.

"But she's the best in her grade at English." Fostina said as she stretched out her legs. "Come on! Let's play netball."

Fostina was playing brilliantly, scoring goal after goal. She spun round, holding the ball. She was not in the right position to score and was looking for someone who was. A little girl bobbed up and down in front of her trying to get the ball.

She knocked the ball from Fostina's hands and ran off with it, laughing.

Constance, the peer leader, had seen what happened. She told the girl to give the ball back. The girl pouted as she did so. "But we want to play too," she said.

"We need Millika," said Grace. "She'd keep the little ones amused, she always does."

"We want Millika," said the little girl. "Millika plays with us."

"Millika is busy," explained Fostina. "She has to study."

The younger children took up a chant, "We want to play. We want to play."

"We want to play too," said Fostina. "But Constance can't referee the netball and play with you at the same time."

"We need another peer leader," said Constance.

"We need Millika," said Fostina.

"Millika! Millika!" the little girl shouted. She pointed across the field. "Millika!" Everyone turned to look. The girl was right. It was Millika. She had walked past the field and was heading towards the village. On her head was a large basket. Fostina ran to catch her up.

"Wait!" she called out, "Millika! Wait!"

Millika turned. Fostina crouched down, panting, in front of her.

"Aren't you coming to Sport in Action?" asked Fostina.

Millika held onto the basket with one hand. "I can't come. I had to study..."

"I know," said Fostina, "but..."

" ...and now I have to go to market to sell this fruit." She lowered the basket. It was full to the brim of mangoes, pineapples, bananas and paw paw.

"But why can't your mum sell the fruit?"

"She's not well," explained Millika. "My sister brought the fruit to school for me."

"Can't your sister sell it then?" pleaded Fostina. "We really need you, Millika."

Millika shook her head. "She has to cook the dinner." She set off along the path, struggling to balance the basket on her head. Fostina grabbed the basket and put it on her own head. She steadied it with one hand. With the other, she grabbed Millika by the wrist and dragged her towards the field.

"What are you doing, Fostina? I need to go to market."

"No," said Fostina. "You need to go to the field. We need you to help with the games."

"But I have to sell this fruit."

"I know," said Fostina, "Come on!" She dragged Millika back along the path to the field. The basket wobbled dangerously, but Fostina kept it on her head. They reached the netball court. The young children crowed round them, tugging at Millika's skirt.

"Millika!" they shouted. "Millika!"

The basket of fruit toppled and fell from Fostina's head, spilling mangoes and paw paw, pineapples and bananas onto the ground. Fostina took one of Millika's hands and waved it in the air.

"Quiet, now," she shouted, "quiet."

Everyone fell silent. They looked at Fostina, waiting for her to speak. Fostina picked up a mango and passed it from one hand to the other.

"We need her here to help us ... " said Fostina. The children nodded. "But if Millika helps us, we need to help Millika too." She held up the mango.

"Millika needs to sell this mango. She needs to sell all the fruits in this basket."

"I'll have a mango," said a girl.

"I'll take a paw paw," said another.

A boy from fourth grade took a bunch of bananas for his grandmother. His friends wanted bananas too. The first graders took pineapples. Soon all the fruit was gone. Those who had no money with them agreed to pay Millika at school the next day. Millika was delighted. She had more money than her mother would usually take at market.

"Can we play, now?" It was the little girl who'd run off with the ball earlier.

"Yes," said Millika. "Let's play."

"Let's play!" the young children shouted.

"Come on, team," said Fostina." Let's play!"

FOOD AND DRINK

Grace, did you know that the Maasai diet mainly includes meat, milk, maize, yoghurt, honey, fat and tree bark?

For breakfast the Maasai people enjoy drinking a cup of sweet tea.

Just a cup of tea? Jackson, we drink tea all the time in the U.K., not just at breakfast time!

For breakfast we have cereal or toast, unless it is a special occasion when we are treated to sausage, bacon and eggs!

Dear friend,

Hi, my name is Chloe, I have brown hair and brown eyes and I am nine years old, how old are you?

I am writing because we want to ask you what life is like in Kenya, We hope to learn lot about your way of life and hopefully you can learn about us too!!!

My favourite food is called Pasta. Pasta is a food which is made out of dough turned into curly shapes. I really like my pasta with tomato sauce mixed with vegetabels in it, What is your favourite food?

I really don't like peas. Peas are small green round circles, I also don't like brussel sprouts :: they taste very horrible.

My Mum is an Aquatarian, that means that she only eats fish and veg but not MEAT!!

I look forward to your reply in letter!

from your friend in England

Chloe Hyde

Dear friend Chloe
My name is Loiparuni. I have two Sisters and
two brothers.
I go to my school every morning and
then I go back to home at evening and then I
help my parents to fech water and cook food
and fech firewood.

I love many animal like cow, sheep, goats, and donkeys.
Cows give us milk sheep give us wood and meat,
donkeys help us to carry heavy loads like water

I ill draw our house

Loiparuni Ikanga

manyatta

Confectionary

Dear Child

Hi!, My name is Hassan. I live in Lancashire, UK. What kind of house do you live in? My hair colour is black, I wonder what kind of hair you have?

In UK we have supermarkets and markets. Also we have things called "convienience stores". They're smaller than supermarkets and markets, but they still sell good things, like newspapers, magazines, and confectionary. My favourite food are pies. I also enjoy "American Style" pancakes. I wonder whats your favourite food?

Thanks
Hassan

Pie

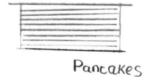
Pancakes

Newspaper

Magazine

Dear, Hassan.

My Name is Thararri Sonkoi. I was born in Loitokitok, Kenya. I live in Kenya.

In Kenya the sky is very dry. What about your Country?
In our school I like to play football I am Man-U fans? What about you?. My hobbies is to play football like Wayne Rooney.

In Kenya Also we have Supermarket and market.

Your faithfully
Thararri Sonkoi.

Hi Friend.

I am Sally and I'm 11 years old. I have brown hair and blue eyes, I have a big family and a lovely house.

At School I have a school dinner and I love them, My faviroute School dinner is . . . . . Pasta bake. Pasta bake is a floury dry dough somtimes covered in a tomatoes sauce or a cheese sauce, I also like pizza, but I dont put ham on my pizza because I am a vegtarian. That means I dont eat animals or fish, but I can eat cheese and eggs and milk and especally fruit and veg. I'm not so keen on tomatoes and beans because they dont taste verry nice. Do you not like anything? Something's though are not verry healthy like milkshakes. Milkshakes are Mik with a fruit taste, but I really like milkshakes, also chocolate is not verry healthy, but is verry sweet and I love it !! I hope to hear from you.

Sally Robson

Dear Sally

I am KApATEA and I'm 13 years old. I have a small family and a lovely manyata house. I have two brother and three sister. My brother is Called Lekioni and LEOLO and My 3 sister are called Nemeha, Naseku and Nagio.

In our Country their is a dry seasean. some area exprence a long drought.

My food is meat, milk and blood. I really like meat and milk. We have a large number of cattle. We graze them.

Do you have cattles?

i hope to hear from you.

Kapatea Lemaroo

Hello,

My name is Kiera, I am 11 years old I like to play outside on my bike, its pink with red flowers, its really fun.

What kind of food do you like? My favourte food is pizza its cruncy, delicous, red with lots of yellow bubbly cheese. When you back a bite its like heaven and you want more. The most ~~horriblest~~ disguiesting food ever is spicy curry, its horrible, its red or brown but the only nice thing about it is the chicken. I dont like it because I hate spicy foods. Do you ever eat crisps, chocolate, are drink cocacola, we do. we call it junk food because its bad for you. What is your favourte meal?

Thank you for reading my letter its nice writting to you.

from Kiera
Bye Bye!!

Dear friends

My name is Susan Kasonta I am 15 years old. I live in Kabwe in a compound and Iam at Katondo basic School in grade 9 B

In Zambia our traditional dish it's nsima we eat nsima twice in a day in the morning and in the evening. Some time we eat nsima with some rerash called rape and small fish which has big head we call them in our Local Laigague has kababa. my favourite fruits are mangoes, bananas oranges.

I would like to know more about you your Family, friends, school and your country.

Yours friend
Susan Kasonta

Hello my name is Jessica June fowler. I am 8 years old. I love Spagetie bolanaze. it's lovley pasta with mints and sause you can get difrent sauses and to get a good texture you can add Veg.

I.m going to ask whats your favedte Meal? because all mine are ribs, Lasanga, Spagetie bolanaze and choclate Cake. I guss youve never heard of them I.ll tell you about them soon.

Ribs is a cows rib they are very nice they have a chinese Souse.

Lasanya is a thek pasta with cheese on it it has mints on it and sause.

Choclate Cake is delishous it has difrent layers of choclate in it and mouth watering Choclate melted.

Thank you for listening
from
Jessica June fowler

Dear Friend

My name is Memory. Iam a Zambian girl aged fifiteen years. My hobbies are reading novels, singing, watching movies, going to church and cooking.

Here in zambia our staple food is nshima We like it very much we eat it with catapiuars in our local language we call it ifishimu. I would like to know you staple food

Our Traditional dish is ifisashi, vegetables like rape, cabbage and nshima. At breakfast I eat tea with sweet potatoes. Do you know sweet potatoes?

Yours Faithfully

Memory

Grandma's Birthday Meal

by Dorothy Massey

"Let's make something special for dinner tonight," said Patience. "A delicious meal for Gran's birthday."

"How about ifisashi?" said Charity. "Gran loves ifisashi."

"But it's Anna's turn to cook tonight," said Patience. "Last time she made ifisashi she burned it."

The sisters laughed, all except the youngest one, Anna, who pouted. "It wasn't my fault it burned," she said.

"You didn't put any water in," said Charity.

"Because you didn't tell me to. You said spinach, ground peanuts, onion, tomatoes and salt. You didn't say water."

"Everyone knows you put water in ifisashi," Charity said.

"You should have told her to add water," said Patience. Anna glared at Charity and wrinkled her nose. Patience smiled at Anna. Anna tried to smile back, but failed.

"I can make a salad," said Anna hopefully. She began to collect the ingredients, putting them into a basket as she did so. "Cucumber, pepper ... garlic ... parsley ... tomatoes ... we've no lemons!"

Charity insisted that salad would not taste right without lemon juice. She suggested meatballs and pasta, but Anna said she didn't like cooking pasta, it always came out too hard or too soft. Patience put a hand on Anna's shoulder and gave it a squeeze. "You make good nshima," she told her.

Anna decided she would make nshima. She scooped some maize flour out of a bag. As she did she heard Gran's voice in her head. *A meal's not a meal without nshima.* She mixed the flour with some cold water to make a smooth paste and put a pan of water onto the stove to boil.

"But what shall we have with the nshima?" asked Charity. "I could make a goat stew."

"We don't have any goat, and anyway, it's Anna's turn," Patience reminded her.

Henry arrived home from school. "What's for dinner?" he asked.

"We haven't decided yet," said Charity.

Henry said they had better hurry , as Gran would be home soon. He wanted to have chicken and chips; Charity groaned and said he always wanted chicken and chips. Then Henry suggested caterpillars but they'd eaten them the day before.

In the kitchen, Anna poured the maize flour paste into the saucepan of boiling water. She stirred with a wooden spoon until the mixture became thick like porridge. Then she left it to simmer.

Charity, Patience and Henry were still arguing in the other room. "Fish," said Patience.

"No, beef," said Henry.

Anna put together the ingredients to make ifisashi; spinach, ground peanuts, salt, an onion and two tomatoes. She filled a jug with water and put it beside the stove. She wouldn't forget to add water this time! In the other room, her sisters and Henry had begun to argue which vegetables they should have.

"Pumpkin," said Henry.

"No, squash," said Charity.

"Pumpkin and squash are both nice," said Patience.

Anna sliced the onion. Her eyes stung and watered, but she wiped them on her sleeve. Then she sliced the tomatoes. She put the tomatoes and onions into a pan with the ground peanuts and a pinch of salt and put them on to boil. She poured in some water. *Not too much, not too little*, she thought. That's good. She lifted the lid of the pan to check the nshima. It was cooking nicely.

"I really think we should have pumpkin," Henry said loudly. "It's Gran's favourite."

"It's not," said Charity. "She loves squash."

"She likes squash and pumpkin," said Patience. "Perhaps squash."

Anna laughed as she added the spinach to the ifisashi and stirred. "Shall I prepare some fruit?" she called through the kitchen door.

"Mangoes," shouted Henry. "I love mangoes."

"It's Gran's birthday, not yours, Henry. Gran likes bananas."

"She likes mangoes too," said Patience. She shouted to Anna, "Do we have mangoes or bananas?"

Anna shouted back that they had both.

While Henry and Patience continued to argue their case for mangoes and bananas, Anna took two pineapples from the fruit basket. She cut off the tops and sliced the pineapples into circles. Then she cut each circle in half and laid the pieces on a plate in a fan shape. *Gran loves pineapple*, she said to herself.

Anna added a little more flour to the nshima and flattened out the lumps with a spoon. She added still more flour until the nshima was just right. *It needs to cook just a little more.* She turned down the heat. *I hope the ifisashi is okay.* She peered into the pan. The ifisashi was perfect. The ingredients had blended together to form a rich, creamy sauce.

Gran walked into the kitchen. "Pineapple," she said. She shut her eyes. "I can smell fresh pineapple."

"Pineapple!" Henry, Charity, then Patience ran into the kitchen.

"Anna," said Patience. "You made a pineapple fan."

"That's not all I made," said Anna proudly. She lifted the pan of ifisashi from the stove and placed it on the table.

"Ifisashi!" said Charity and Patience.

"My favourite," said Henry.

"And mine," said Gran.

"Happy birthday, Gran," said Anna.

"We cooked you a special dinner," said Charity.

"Anna cooked you a special dinner," said Patience. "All we did was argue."

LET'S SAY THANK YOU!

We have come to the end of the school day
We have come to the end of the school day

Let's say thank you to those who taught
us how to read and write.

We have come to the end of the school day
We have come to the end of the school day

Let us say thank you to those who taught us
to read and write.

This song is sung by schoolchildren in Nigeria; I and many other children used to sing this song after school everyday.

I really enjoyed singing it and it should be sung loudly, to express how thankful or appreciative we were to our helpers and teachers.

On the opposite page you can see the song and the words in Igbo language, which is not spoken very much any more and might disappear in the future. Sad, isn't it?

- Ifeoma Onyefulu, author of *A for Africa*

MAASAI CULTURE

The Maasai are known as pastoralists. Pastoralists are people who keep livestock, like sheep, goat and cows, and move around to find good pastures. The Maasai lifestyle used to involve lots of moving around to find new grass for their cattle. This lifestyle is called nomadic. Nowadays the Maasai are semi-nomadic, which means that they do not travel great distances with their cattle, but tend to stay in the same area where they build homes to live in.

You won't find the Maa language in a dictionary or a book because it is only a spoken language. This makes Maa an endangered language. Although there are many different ways of speaking Maa in Kenya and Tanzania, all the versions are very similar. The Maa language that is presented in this book is based upon the dialect spoken in Southern Kenya. All languages are important as they represent different cultures and how different people see the world.

FASCINATING FACTS

The Maasai believe that the sun and moon are married. When a new moon appears the Maasai throw a twig or stone with their left hand and ask for a long life and strength.

Celebrations for births, initiations and moving up in age sets for boys are big events in Maasai culture. The warriors decorate themselves with chalk and red colouring. Before the celebration, a goat is sacrificed and the best part (the liver) is then given to the elders to eat.

There are three peaks of Mount Kenya that are named after famous Maasai. These are Lenana and his sons Merishi and Mbatian, who were all important Maasai leaders in the 20th Century.

In Maa, months of the year are named after the expected weather conditions. For example, March is known as the Month of Plenty due to the heavy rain, which means the grass will grow, whilst July is known as the Month of Quarrels because of the lack of rain.

Once upon a time, the Maasai believed that the sky and earth were one. Their god Enkai lived on earth but one day a Dorobo hunter shot an arrow at him and made him angry. Enkai then separated the earth and sky and went to live permanently in the sky.

The Maasai believe that all cattle on earth were given to them by their god, Enkai. Enkai is known as the black god when he brings the rain and tall grass, and the red god when there is no rain.

THE LIFE OF MAASAI CHILDREN

Enkang is what the Maasai call the homestead, where the children live with their mothers in their Enkaji, a traditional Maasai house.

Maasai girls and boys have very different upbringings. Take a look at the different, but equally important, journeys the children take into adulthood...

Girls are aged fourteen when their initiation takes place.

Girls move out of their mother's home and are taught by older women about housekeeping, marriage and caring for babies.

Girls then have a Ceremony and become women. This then means they are ready for marriage.

It is a woman's role to build their houses. They use soil, cow dung, grass and timber.

© Kate Johnson

120

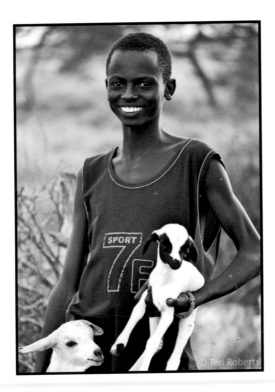

At the age of 13/14, boys go through their Initiation and have their heads shaved

They then move to a Manyatta (a special kind of village) and become a Junior Warrior.

Boys then begin to grow back their hair and start to look after cattle.

Around ten years later, they join the Enkiguena (a council of elders) and then they can become Senior Elders.

In their early twenties, boys have a ceremony called Eunoto. This is really important as the Senior Elders decide whether it is time for the Junior Warriors to become Junior Elders.

After this, they are allowed to marry and own cattle.

Did you know….?
When boys have had their initiation they put on a long, blanket lined garment and carry special bows and arrows that have been blunted and made safe. The boy will use these to shoot at all the young girls he meets to show that he is interested in them!

My Experience of the Maasai

by Therese Green

The Maasai Tribe:

There are around 42 different tribes living in Kenya, of which the Maasai are the most famous. I stayed at the Maasai Centre for Field studies, which can be found in the heart of Maasai land in southern Kenya near the border of Tanzania and in full view of Mount Kilimanjaro. Here you can learn about Maasai culture from the local men and women, but it was the Maasai children whose stories I really wanted to hear. The children have lots of dreams about their future. They also value their traditional way of life and are concerned by how it is being affected by the modern world.

Maasai Values:

Cattle – such as cows and goats – are central to Maasai identity. They are important for wealth and status. Before the introduction of free education in 2003, the boys would gain responsibility by looking after livestock. From the age of five they would care for a kid or a lamb, and then between seven and eight they would look after calves. From ages eight to ten they would tend some goats or sheep until, finally, from the age of eleven to twelve they would herd cows. Because children now go to school, this happens less often, usually after school or at weekends.

Children are now described as important as their cattle to Maasai parents because of the benefits that education might bring them. I often found parents selling their cows so that they could afford to send their children to school.

Respect:

The Maasai respect their elders by lowering their head forward to be touched by them. It is only the girls, boys and women who lower their heads; the men shake hands when they meet. Generosity and hospitality are maintained by welcoming any passer-by into the home and it is customary to offer food and drink. The Maasai community share the responsibility of each person's wellbeing and social development. When I asked the children what they really valued most about the Maasai culture, the most important aspects to them were respect and discipline.

Western vs. Tradition:

The children wore western clothes and were banned from wearing traditional dress or jewellery, and having elongated ears at school. The only time they dressed traditionally was to give a dance and song show.

The Maasai children expressed a desire to use their education to help modernise the Maasai community. They wanted to 'bring change to our society', 'develop our society by educating people', and 'help to fight poverty'. Many talked about becoming a teacher, a doctor, nurse, a member of parliament or a pilot.

Maa is the language of the Maasai. At school it was not encouraged – it was sidelined by the children's wish to learn Kiswahili and English. People in Kenya are starting to associate speaking Maa with not being educated or 'learned'.

One child, Silole, said to me: '(The) only thing I like is talking Maasai language because I can't do all the steps of the Maasai culture, putting on Maasai clothes [sic].'

The eagerness of the children to become educated could be positive for the Maasai's future. However, while learning opens the mind, it would be sad to lose the values the children have learned through the Maasai culture. As well as the Maasai gaining from education, wouldn't it be positive if other cultures, including those from the West, could benefit, by studying traditional Maasai values such as respect and a sense of community?

KENYA

by Jasper Green

I look into the eyes of the poor and I feel their pain
If anyone else were there too, I'm sure they'd feel the same
Maasai children making their own homemade games
We complain about the weather, they're lucky when it rains

On the equator, the large sun blazing like fire
Sets behind Kilimanjaro, turning the sky from orange to sapphire
No light pollution resulting in a solution of the Milky Way, galaxies and stars
Without a telescope, you can see Venus and sometimes you can see Mars

Many different creatures roaming the vast land
Some of which are endangered and require a helping hand
The large, green and golden land being ruled by the giant five
Dominant and grand beasts, making the most of their time whilst they're alive

The Kenyan people have a certain warmth about their outgoing personality
The type that would brighten up a situation of awkward banality
Many peaceful, happy people make up their communities
Then they come together to form one big family called Kenya in unity

There's still lots more to be said about this great nation
A fantastic place full of creativity and variation

THE MAA LANGUAGE

The Maa Language is not a written language and so different Maasai people may say words in different ways. The words here are how our Maasai friend James says them...

Children bow their heads to show respect to adults.
And the adult puts their hand on the head as a greeting to say hello.

© Adam Beazley

When two women say hello the first woman says, "Takwenya," and the second woman replies, "Ikuo."

When two men say hello the first man says, "Supa," and the second man replies, "Ipa."

Isla Choyce, Coates Primary School

LEARN TO SPEAK MAA

GREETINGS

English	Maa	Sounds like...
Goodbye	Sere	Seray
Goodnight	Rraga Esidai	Escranya essayday
Hello (to a man)	Supa	Soopa
Hello (to a woman)	Takwenya	Tackwenya
How are you?	Supa?	Soopa
How much?	Iropiyanai aja?	Iropiyanai aja
I am from ...	Ainguaa ...	Ainguaa ...
I am ...years old	Aata nanu ilarin...	Arrta nannoo Illarin ...
I'm cold	Eirobi	Ayrowbi
I'm fine	Aserian	Asserien
I'm happy	Ashipa	Ashibba
I'm hot	Eirowya	Ay erooya
I'm hungry	Aata esumash	Arrta essayoomash
I'm ill	Amuei	Armoowee
I'm sad	Aisinanuo	Assee narneeyou
I'm thirsty	Aata enjure	Arrta engooray
I'm tired	Anaura	Anaoora
My name is ...	Aaji enkarna	Arryee Enkarna
No	Ah -ah	Ah –ah
Please	Aatoomono	Arrtoomowno
Reply to greeting hello (f)	Ikuo	Eequo
Reply to greeting hello (m)	Ipa	Eepa
Thank you	Ashe	Ashay
Where are you from?	Kai-inguaa?	Kai-inguaa
Where's the toilet?	Koree enkaji ootonat?	Koray enkagee ontow nat
Yes	Aee	aay

English	Maa	Sounds like...

ANIMALS

English	Maa	Sounds like...
Baboon	Oltulal	Oltoolal
Cat	Enpaka	Enpakka
Cattle	Eramatare	Elamarparay
Cow	Enkiteng	Enkeeteng
Dog	Oldia	Oldeeya
Donkey	Osikiria	Osikeerria
Giraffe	Ormeut	Ormayoot
Goat	Enkine	Enkeenay
Lion	Olowuaru	Olloowaru
Sheep	Enkerr	En ke

SCHOOL

English	Maa	Sounds like...
Blackboard	Enkibao	Enkibowoo
Friends	Ilshorueti	Inchoorooetti
Playtime	Esaa-enkiguran	Essarr - Enkigooran
Pupil	Enkerai esukuul	Enkarra yee esserkool
Schoolbook	Enbuku esukuul	Embookoo esserkool
Teacher	Ormalimui	Ormarlee mwee

HOBBIES

English	Maa	Sounds like...
Dancing	Osing'olio	Osing goleo
Football	Empira	Empeerra
Games	Enkiguran	Enkeegooran
Singing	Eranyare	Elan yaray

English	Maa	Sounds like...
HOME		
Bed	Erruat	Ayhoolat
Brother	Olalashe	Olala shay
Chair	Olorika	Ullorika
Cup	Embilaoni	Embeela oti
Father	Papa	Paapa
Fire	Enkima	Enkeema
Fork	Enkijiko oolala	Enkinyooko oolala
Granddad	Nkakuyia	Ungarkooyar
Grandma	Kokoo	Koko
House	Enkaji	Elnkarji
Knife	Enkalem	Enkalem
Mother	Yieyio	Yeiyo
Sister	Enkanashe	Aingarnashay
Spoon	Enkijiko	Enkinyooko
Table	Emesa	Aymessa

English	Maa	Sounds like...
FOOD		
Breakfast	Shai enkakenya	Shy ee engakenya
Lunch	Endeaa edama	Endar endemma
Maize	Ilpayek	Impieyek
Market	Osingira	Oh singirra
Meat	Inkiri	Enkirri
Milk	Kule	Koolay
Tea (drink)	Shaai	Shy ee
Tea (meal)	Shai eteipa	Shy ee aytaypa

Maasai Centre for Field Studies

The Maasai Centre for Field Studies can be found in the heart of Kimana in Kenya.

The Centre itself is situated in the middle of the Kuku group ranch, which is surrounded by all sorts of animals that can be seen on local safari, including zebras, ostriches and even elephants!

The Centre is a place for research and education, run by a Maasai community and the University of Central Lancashire in England.

Anybody can visit the Maasai Centre, from backpackers and wildlife fans to universities and schools.

As the centre is a non-profit organisation, the money they make is used to support the Kuku community, including educational and environmental projects.

The Maasai Centre is very eco-friendly: all the power used is solar energy, there are recycling schemes for waste, and the water is piped in straight from the springs of Mount Kilimanjaro.

There are English speaking members of staff at the centre who are teachers and researchers with lots of experience. They are also experts on the local environment and can teach visitors all they could want to know about local wildlife, culture and even some of the Maa language!

The accommodation is made up of several large tents on a solid base with a thatched roof to protect visitors from any weather. There's even a library, with books about the local area and Africa in general.

To find out more about this superb place and how to get involved, please visit: www.maasaicentre.org

Jasper Green, 12, writes about his own experiences of the Maasai Centre

I have been to the Maasai Centre four times and when I'm there I enjoy socialising with the locals and observing the natural environment. I also enjoys days out on safari. I like elephants. It is a very well known animal in the area. They relate very much to human nature, for example with the way they grieve and their mother and child relationships.

I have many friends there, all of which are different from each other, but are also different from my friends at home. My Kenyan friends take a lot less for granted but they are still very happy children. Their school facilities are very run down but they still make do. Their play areas are on the open savannah. They are more enthusiastic about education than my friends back at home!

My favourite thing about the Kenyan way of life is that they adapt to the natural environment around them, reducing their carbon footprints. Also, everyone knows everyone; they're all one big family.

SOUTH LAKES WILD ANIMAL PARK

We don't just talk about conservation...
We get out there and do it!

South Lakes Wild Animal Park opened in 1994, allowing people the chance to see some of the planet's rarest and most amazing animals. South Lakes Wild Animal Park is dedicated to conserving the thousands of species of animals that face extinction. They take part in conservation projects all over the world, including their two international charities The Sumatran Tiger Trust and The Wildlife Protection Foundation.

Giraffe Conservation – Niger, West Africa

Amongst other conservation projects in Africa, South Lakes Wild Animal Park is working to help the giraffes in Niger, which have been the victims of hunting, poaching, and loss of habitat. In 1996, in the region of Dallol Bosso near Naimey (capital of Niger), there were only 41 giraffes left. The Peralta giraffes of Niger are critically endangered and are the last giraffes left in West Africa.

The ASGN is the Association to Safeguard the Giraffes of Niger, which was created in order to protect the giraffes and their habitat. They also aim to improve the lives of the local communities, in order to prevent conflict between the people and the giraffes. South Lakes Wild Animal Park and The Wildlife Protection Foundation has supported the ASGN since 2005, along with Zoo de Doue-la-Fontaine (France).

Amongst many other conservation approaches the ASGN offers villagers cereals in exchange for planting trees. These trees can be used as food for the giraffes, which is important as many of the plants the giraffes eat cannot survive Niger's common droughts. The ASGN works with the local communities to increase awareness of sustainable development solutions and change their perceptions of the giraffe.

In 2008, 185 giraffes were recorded in Niger thanks to their hard work and dedication!

To see how you can help the giraffes in Niger please visit www.wildlifeprotection.info

Letters to Africa would like to thank South Lakes Wild Animal Park for their donation of the 'Keeper for a Day' prize to Jack Sagar, winner of our letter-writing competition.

South Lakes Wild Animal Park
Crossgates, Dalton-in-Furness, Cumbria LA15 8JR
Telephone:01229 466086   Fax: 01229 461310
Email: office@wildanimalpark.co.uk

SPORT IN ACTION

Sport In Action (SIA) is a non-governmental organisation (NGO) whose purpose is to improve people's quality of life through sport and recreational activities. Founded in 1998, SIA was the first Zambian sports NGO. With Sport for Development (the use of sport as a tool for social change) as its underlying principle, SIA positively impacts the lives of thousands of children throughout 24 districts in Zambia.

SIA staff and volunteers work with more than 160,000 children each week, many of whom come from challenging backgrounds. Through this work lives have been transformed due to knowledge enhancement in the area of health life skills, behavioural change towards both family and peers and improvement in sporting abilities.

A MESSAGE ABOUT SPORT IN ACTION. FROM DOROTHY MASSEY, THE AUTHOR OF LET'S PLAY

Sport in Action is an organisation set up in 1998 with the aim of improving people's lives through sport and games. In Zambia, staff and volunteers work in 24 districts with over 160,000 children every week. Many of these children come from challenging backgrounds. Some are orphans, some have disabilities and others are homeless or have difficult family lives. The programmes teach them to lead healthy lives. They also provide fun, and an opportunity to learn sports and life skills.

Sport in Action's motto is 'Active, healthy and better living for all.' Children play sports such as football and netball as well as traditional Zambian games involving chants and dances, board games and sport. Important messages about keeping safe and healthy are taught directly through these activities. The organisation provides training and materials for teachers as well as camps, tournaments and festivals.

Let's Play was inspired by my visit in March and April 2010 to Kabwe in Northern Zambia with students and staff from the University of Central Lancashire's Right to Play module. These students worked with Sport in Action staff and volunteers to provide activities in a number of projects linked to schools in the Kabwe area. The module has been so successful, the programme leader plans to extend it to other countries in the future. I was lucky to see for myself how much the children and young people learned and how much they enjoyed themselves. Many children walked miles to join in, some with younger brothers and sisters on their backs. As the Sport in Action leaders said, 'Zambian children love to play.'

Author Biographies

Lauren St John was born in Gatooma, Rhodesia, now Kadoma, Zimbabwe. She is the author of the award-winning children's series, The Whilte Giraffe, Dolphin Song, The Last Leopard and The Elephant's Tale.

Mary Hoffman is the bestselling author of Amazing Grace. Her novel, Troubador, was nominated for the 2010 Carnegie Medal. She lives in Oxforshire with her husband and three cats.

Dorothy Massey loves writing and encouraging others to write too! When one of her stories for children won the Pinestein Press Things that go Bump competition she was asked to write three short stories, The Ghost Twin Tales which appeared in the book, Mini Mysteries and Kooky Spookies. Another competition winning story, Munch the Storytelling Cow, was recorded as a podcast by celebrity TV presenter, Gail Porter.

Victoria Todd is currently studying an MA in Writing for Children, and will begin doctoral study this year. She is the first UCLan student to have a creative writing piece accepted by Diffusion, UCLan's journal for undergraduate research.

Ifeoma Onyefulu was born in Nigeria. She is an author and a photographer. She has written 15 children's books, the most popular of which is A is For Africa, used in schools in England and in America. She is currently working on two more books set in Ethiopia.

THE PUBLISHERS WOULD LIKE TO THANK

Katondo Upper Basic School, Twafwane Community School and Sport Academy, Mellor St Mary's CE Primary School, Kabwe Trust Basic School in Zambia, Enkaji Naibor Primary School and Enkii Primary School in Kenya.

Caitlin Austin and Jack Sagar from Farington Primary School, Abbie Cayton, Isabel Cockerham and Jessica June Fowler from Woodleigh Primary School, Elsa Newell from Withnell Fold Primary , Emma Rowley, Hassan Jawad, Jessica Kelly, Jordan Hindle, Kiera Flanagan, Olivia Schofield and Thomas from Hippings Methodist School, Alice Singleton, Ellie Dent and Sammy Jo Milner from John Cross CE Primary School, Ben Anderton from St Josephs Primary School, Sonia Higginson and Zoe Lakeland from St Oswalds Primary School, Emily Taylor from Higher Walton, Amy Crossdale, Amber Metherell, Andrew Morris, Chloe Hyde, Jonathon George Taylor, Sally Robson and Toby Gilmore from Ribby with Wrea C. E. Primary School, Isla Choyce from Coates Lane Primary School, Emily Harris from Leyland Methodist Primary School, and all other participating schools and pupils.

Cliff Olsson, Jackson Kilinga, James Ole Maantoi and the Maasai centre staff, Jake Hope, Jasper Green, Joe Craig, Karen Brewer, Mark Toogood, Steve Speed, Therese Green, Yvonne Lancaster, Dawn Archer, Lyndsey Gibson, Katerina Finnis, Luana Cirstea, Magda Szpyrka, Kate Johnson, Teri-Adele Roberts, Adam Beazley, Gemma Nolan, Paula Murray, Sarah El-Taki, Becky Robinson, the Chileshe family, Sylvester Mbewe and family, Richard and Ben Massey.

Thank you!
Becky Forster, Emily Linnett, Emily Williams,
Fran Hazlehurst, Rachel Winterbottom and Toni Comer